U.S. Military Forces

U.S. COAST GUARD

JULIA GARSTECKI

BLACK RABBIT BOOKS

Bolt is published by Black Rabbit Books
P.O. Box 3263, Mankato, Minnesota, 56002
www.blackrabbitbooks.com

Jennifer Besel, editor; Michael Sellner, interior designer;
Catherine Cates, cover designer; Omay Ayres, photo researcher

Library of Congress Cataloging-in-Publication Data
Names: Garstecki, Julia, author.
Title: U.S. Coast Guard / by Julia Garstecki.
Description: Mankato, Minnesota : Bolt is published by Black Rabbit Books, [2021]
Series: Bolt. U.S. military forces | Includes bibliographical references and index.
Audience: Ages 8-12 | Audience: Grades 4-6
Summary: "Learn about the powerful soldiers who make up the U.S. Coast Guard, including what they do and the training it takes to become one."— Provided by publisher.
Identifiers: LCCN 2019037821 (print) | LCCN 2019037822 (ebook)
ISBN 9781623102982 (hardcover) | ISBN 9781644663943 (paperback)
ISBN 9781623103927 (ebook)
Subjects: LCSH: United States. Coast Guard—Juvenile literature.
Classification: LCC VG53 .G37 2021 (print) | LCC VG53 (ebook)
DDC 363.28/60973—dc23
LC record available at https://lccn.loc.gov/2019037821
LC ebook record available at https://lccn.loc.gov/2019037822

Image Credits

coastguard.dodlive.mil: Petty Officer 3rd Class Luke Clayton / U.S. Coast Guard, 15 (b); commons.wikimedia.org / uscg.mil: Mark Farmer / U.S. Coast Guard, 24–25; defense.gov: U.S. Coast Guard, 1, 4–5, 6; dodlive.mil: Petty Officer 2nd Class Walter Shinn / U.S. Coast Guard, 9 (t); dvidshub.net: U.S. Coast Guard, 26–27; navy.mil: Mass Communication Specialist 1st Class Erik Hoffmann / U.S. Navy, 15 (t); news.uscg.mil: U.S. Coast Guard, Cover (main); Shutterstock: irin-k, 12–13 (dots); Neuevector, Cover (wings); objectsforall, 28–29 (jacket); Peter Titmuss, 29 (main); uscg.mil: Petty Officer 1st Class Luke Pinneo / U.S. Coast Guard, 9 (b); Petty Officer 1st Class Melissa Leake / U.S. Coast Guard, 16 (b); Ross Ruddell / U.S. Coast Guard, 32; U.S. Coast Guard, 9 (c), 10, 11, 16 (t), 18–19, 20 (b), 31; usni.org: USNI News, 3, 23; work.uscg.mil: U.S. Coast Guard, 14, 20 (t); Every effort has been made to contact copyright holders for material reproduced in this book. Any omissions will be rectified in subsequent printings if notice is given to the publisher.

Contents

CHAPTER 1

To Protect and Serve

In 2018, a hurricane blasted North Carolina. It left behind dangerous flooding. Deep water trapped people in their homes. But the U.S. Coast Guard came to their rescue. Pilots flew helicopters over the flooded areas. Members in the choppers lowered down to the water. They lifted people and pets into the choppers. Then they flew them to safety.

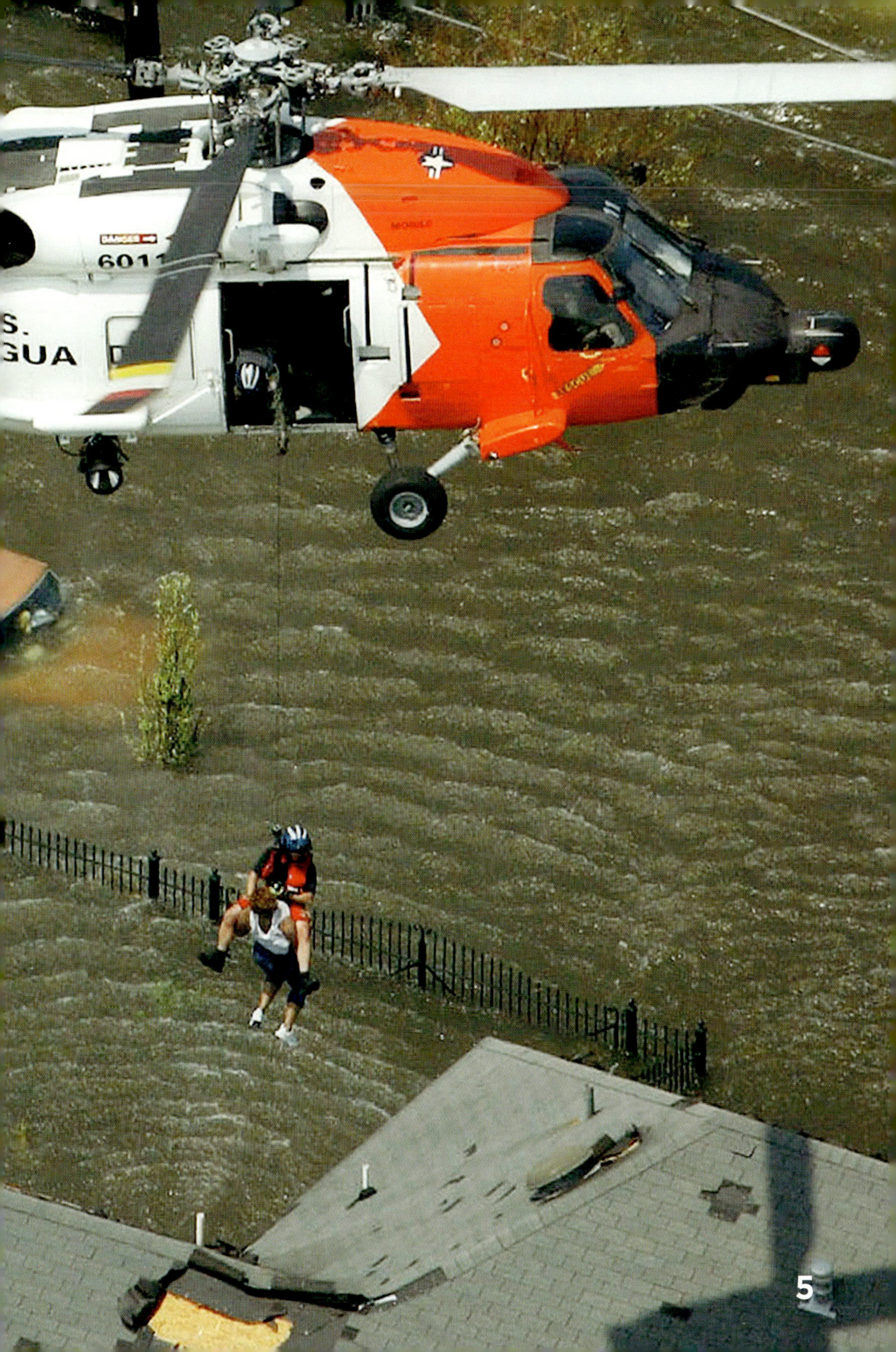
DANGER
6011
S.
GUA

BERGE BOSTON
US
COAST

Important Roles

Rescues are just one of the U.S. Coast Guard's jobs. Members also stop drug **smugglers**. They clean up waterways. And they defend **ports**. They are always ready to keep the United States safe.

CHAPTER 2

Training

It takes a lot of training to be a Coast Guard member. Every member starts with basic training. The training lasts eight weeks. **Recruits** prove they are physically able to do the job. They also learn to use weapons, fight fires, and do rescues.

Recruits also study military rules and history.

PHYSICAL
TRAINING

RESCUE
TRAINING

FIREFIGHTING

U.S. COAST GUARD

After Basic

Recruits who pass basic training go on to their **assignments**. They serve all around the country. But they don't stop training. Members continue to take classes. These classes help them become better at their jobs.

U.S. COAST GUARD BASES

Members work from bases all around the United States.

Canada
Massachusetts
Connecticut
Rhode Island
Maryland
New Jersey
Ohio
West Virginia
Virginia
North Carolina
Oklahoma
Alabama
Florida

CHAPTER 3

Jobs and Missions

The Coast Guard trains people for all kinds of jobs. Some members protect wildlife in the water. Others keep ships safe from pirate attacks.

One of the Coast Guard's biggest jobs is protecting ports. Ships bring items into the United States every day. The Coast Guard protects ports from enemies.

Other Coast Guard Jobs

rescuing boats at sea

mapping icebergs

stopping boats carrying drugs

The Coast Guard patrols more than 100,000 miles (160,934 kilometers) of coastline and inland waterways.

Rescues

The Coast Guard is also called on in emergencies. Members lower on cables from helicopters. They can rescue people in the ocean. They can also be lowered onto cliffs to rescue hikers.

U.S. COAST GUARD

By the Numbers

about **19,790**

number of search and rescue cases the Guard has in one year

about **41,000**

number of active members

10

average number of lives Coast Guard members save each day

more than

1,000 pounds

(454 kilograms)

average weight of drugs the Guard collects each day

OIL RIG

Cleanup

The Coast Guard also works to protect the oceans. Some members work with oil companies. They make sure ships and **oil rigs** don't leak. But oil spills do happen. The Coast Guard helps organize the cleanup.

CHAPTER 4

Gear and Weapons

The Coast Guard uses many kinds of ships. Icebreakers smash ice chunks in cold waters. These boats often carry scientists doing experiments.

Cutters are useful boats. They have room for crew to live onboard. The Guard uses them for rescues and other jobs. Some have spy equipment. Members can use these boats to search for illegal drugs.

Some cutters have cannons and machine guns.

Alex Haley

The *Alex Haley* is a U.S. Coast Guard cutter. It's used in the waters around Alaska.

WEAPONS

2 Mk 38 25-mm cannons

2 .50-caliber machine guns

Line-Throwing Guns

Rescuing boats isn't easy. Sometimes the Coast Guard needs to pull a boat. Members use line-throwing guns. The gun shoots a towing line across rough seas. Then the Coast Guard ship can drag the broken ship to safety.

Always Ready

The Coast Guard has protected the United States since 1790. It watches the United States' water areas. And members are prepared for rescues. It is always ready.

FURUNO
45605

assignment (uh-SIGN-ment)—a position, post, or office to which one is assigned

base (BAYS)—a place where military operations begin

inland (IN-land)—part of the interior of a country

oil rig (OYL RIG)—a structure that has equipment attached to it for drilling and removing oil from the ground

port (PORT)—a harbor town or city where ships take on or deliver cargo

recruit (ri-KROOT)—a newcomer to a group or field of activity

smuggler (SMUG-lur)—a person who brings items into a country secretly and against the law

LEARN MORE

BOOKS

Abdo, Kenny. *United States Coast Guard.* U.S. Armed Forces. Minneapolis: Abdo Zoom, 2019.

Grack, Rachel. *U.S. Coast Guard.* Serving Our Country. Mankato, MN: Amicus, 2019.

Mitchell, P. P. *Join the Coast Guard.* US Armed Forces. New York: Gareth Stevens Publishing, 2018.

WEBSITES

Serving in the U.S. Coast Guard
www.gocoastguard.com/

United States Coast Guard
www.britannica.com/topic/United-States-Coast-Guard

United States Coast Guard
www.uscg.mil/

INDEX